# SUPERGUIDES

# DOGS

## WENDY BOORER

KINGFISHER BOOKS

Kingfisher Books, Grisewood & Dempsey Ltd,
Elsley House, 24–30 Great Titchfield Street,
London W1P 7AD

This edition published in 1989 by Kingfisher Books.
Material in this book was first published in 1981
in the Kingfisher Guide series.

© Kingfisher Books 1981, 1989

British Library Cataloguing in Publication Data
Boorer, Wendy
    Dogs.
    1. Livestock; Dogs. Breeds
    I. Title II. Series
    636.7'1

    ISBN 0-86272-486-4

All illustrations by John Francis except p.4,
Bernard Robinson

Edited by Stuart Cooper
Designed by Millions Design
Printed in Hong Kong

# CONTENTS

# INTRODUCTION

The origin of the domestic dog still remains uncertain though most scientists believe that it had wolf-like ancestors as it displays many behavioural and structural resemblances to the wolf. It has also been shown that wolves can be interbred with domestic dogs to produce fertile and tameable offspring. The jackal too has been cited as an ancestor, though the evidence is slight. Another theory is that the dog has more than one ancestral form, with jackals, wolves and others having all played a part. This would account in part for the wide variation in the shape and size of breeds. Unfortunately, archeological evidence is lacking, for the area where domestication is thought to have taken place, south-western Asia, has been little researched in this respect.

## MAN'S BEST FRIEND

When domestication of the dog took place is equally speculative. It is thought that the first tentative relationship between man and dog began about 20,000 years ago or even earlier. Domestication was a long, slow process, and probably evolved in primitive cultures in different parts of the world and at different stages of development.

The reasons for the early association between man and dog are more apparent. Primitive man, preying on grazing animals, left a trail of rotting waste which would attract canine packs. Following the nomadic hunting tribes would become a way of life for the wild dog and, as man began to settle, he could begin to appreciate the scavengers who kept down the stench and flies and gave warning of the approach of anything unusual. Both canine and human groups began to hunt together. There is evidence from France that at a very early date men and wild dogs combined to stampede herds of horses over cliffs. However, it was not until the dog began to track ahead and hold at bay wounded game, that man began to realize how useful the dog could become.

*Similarities of structure and behaviour suggest that the dog is descended from wolf-like ancestors.*

## WORKING DOGS

The earliest of pictorial and written records from the Middle East show that specialization into types of dog suited to a particular function was already well under way. The ancient Egyptians were skilled animal breeders keeping many animals now regarded as completely wild. While Neolithic Man was still using flint axes in Europe, there were already several distinct types of hunting dog being bred by the Egyptians and Sumerians. These were mainly sighthounds to catch game on the open plains. By the time of the Greek civilization, a variety of scent hounds were bred and kept. These were capable of following trails through thick vegetation where visibility was poor.

Man's ability to select and regulate breeding for a functional purpose helped to fix a breed type. Leisure and money enabled the nobility through the ages to develop various hunting hounds for its own use and amusement, and some toy dogs probably received the same care and attention in the courts of Europe. These dogs were valuable and were taken along the commercial routes of the world as trading commodities. In contrast, the rural working breeds, the sheep and herding dogs, were protected from outside influences by their virtual isolation. They were of little value except to their masters as lack of communication meant that each agricultural community developed a distinct type of its own for a particular job.

## SHOW DOGS

Throughout most of man's history, dogs have been kept for a working purpose. The growth of various breeds was dictated by man's needs and many of them spread along the trade routes, or with invading armies or waves of immigrant settlers. Breeds have become extinct as a result of technological advances which have made some working dogs redundant. A new element entered into this with the advent of dog shows in the 19th century.

# PARTS OF A DOG

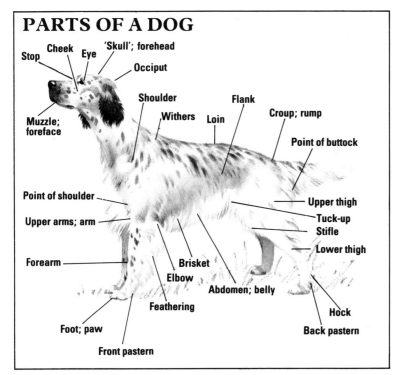

Stop
Cheek
Eye
'Skull'; forehead
Occiput
Shoulder
Flank
Loin
Croup; rump
Muzzle; foreface
Withers
Point of buttock
Point of shoulder
Upper arms; arm
Upper thigh
Tuck-up
Stifle
Lower thigh
Forearm
Brisket
Elbow
Abdomen; belly
Feathering
Hock
Foot; paw
Back pastern
Front pastern

Dogs began to be kept for competition, with breeders striving to produce an ideal whose worth they could measure against other dogs in the show ring.

The first organized dog show in the world was held in the UK in 1859. The idea became established and led to a controlling body, the Kennel Club, being founded in 1873. Since then, dog showing has grown in popularity throughout the world, with each country having its own authority. Kennel Clubs have three main functions. They licence and regulate all shows held within their jurisdiction. They record the pedigrees of all dogs registered with them, and dogs not registered cannot be shown. They also publish the standard for each breed, a written blueprint for the ideal type. Unfortunately, these standards are not necessarily the same from one country to another. In particular, colour, weight and size may differ. The weights and sizes quoted in this book are mainly drawn from the English Kennel Club standards and are the maximum for a male animal. Bitches are almost invariably smaller. The height given is the measurement from the dog's withers to the ground.

For administrative convenience, Kennel Clubs also arrange breeds into groups. These are also not standardized worldwide. Classification of dog breeds is not easy as the relationship between many of them is not clear. Attempts to subdivide dogs by function, the original work for which they were bred, are not entirely satisfactory, and neither are those which subdivide by form, linking supposed anatomical relationships. The grouping in this book is a somewhat uneasy compromise between the two.

# GLOSSARY

**apricot** a pinkish-fawn colour
**badger** colouring of mixed white, brown and grey
**blaze** a white mark down the centre of the forehead
**blue** a bluish-grey colouring
**blue merle** a silvery-blue flecked and dappled with black
**brindle** black stripes on a paler background, or mingling of black hair with a lighter colour
**bring to bay** force an animal to stand and turn rather than flee
**coursing** a sport which matches sighthounds against a speedy quarry, e.g. two greyhounds against a hare
**crop** to cut off the ear of a dog to leave an erect, pointed, remnant
**croup** the rump
**dewclaws** a rudimentary pad and claw found a little way up the inside of the front and hindlegs
**dock** to cut off all or part of the tail
**draught dog** one used for haulage
**earth** burrow or underground home of vermin
**feathering** fringes of long hair on the ears, backs of the legs and tail
**field trials** competitions whereby the abilities of gundogs are assessed

**flush** force out into the open
**foreface** the part of the head between the eyes and the nose
**give tongue** yelp or bay when hunting
**grizzle** an iron-grey colour with a mixture of black hair
**harlequin** a white dog patched with colour (usually black)
**hock** hindleg joint corresponding to the human ankle
**lay back** receding nose of a short-faced breed
**mask** darker colouring on the muzzle and cheeks
**merle** *see* blue merle
**moult** dropping of the old coat to allow for the growth of new hair
**nose** scenting powers
**overshot** the upper teeth projecting a long way in front of the lower teeth
**particolour** two clear and distinct colours on a single animal
**pedigree** a dog whose ancestry is known and written down; the form on which such an ancestry is written
**pied** a white dog marked with irregular patches of one other colour
**point** to indicate the presence of a game scent by standing rigidly
**purebred** having ancestors of the same breed
**recognition** the acceptance by a

Kennel Club or other national canine authority that a breed is purebred
**roan** an even intermingling of two colours to give a mottled effect
**sable** black-tipped hair overlaying a lighter colour
**scissor bite** where the upper teeth fit closely over the lower in front
**self-coloured** one colour all over
**set** to indicate the presence of a game scent by standing motionless
**shed** *see* moult
**sighthound** a dog that hunts by sight rather than scent
**solid-coloured** *see* self-coloured
**standard** a written description of a breed ideal
**stripping out** pulling out or thinning the coat
**stud book** record of the breeding of a number of dogs
**tricolour** a mixture of three defininte colours in the coat, usually black, white and tan
**type** the characteristics which make up that particular breed
**undershot** where the lower teeth project in front of the upper ones
**wall-eye** a blue or marbled eye
**whole-coloured** *see* self-coloured
**withers** where the neck joins the back; usually the point of the shoulder blades can be felt there

# SHEEP AND CATTLE DOGS

In most areas of the world where sheep and cattle have played a part in man's economy, dogs have been used to guard, move and control them. Techniques of shepherding and cattle raising have varied from country to country. Different predators, terrains, and methods of husbandry have led to a wide variety of breeds being produced. Shepherding has often been a lonely and isolated job and lack of communication with the outside world has also led to the development of many local types of dog, each tailored to the specific needs of the area. Some dogs in this group are far removed from their working past. Others are still primarily working dogs whose energy and drive make them totally unsuitable as pets. Many are highly intelligent and responsive to training, able to form the closest of relationships with man. For this reason they have adapted easily in the modern world to a wide variety of roles other than shepherding.

Shetland Sheepdog

Old English Sheepdog

Bearded Collie

## SHETLAND SHEEPDOG
The barren, windswept Shetland Islands are widely known for the ponies and sheepdogs that bear their name. Both the Shetland Pony and the Shetland Sheepdog are diminutive versions of their mainland relatives. The small working farm dog began to attract much attention in the early 1900s. As well as being an attractive size, these dogs were hardy, sweet-natured and intelligent, though not as handsome as their modern descendants. Sables, tricolours and merles are the usual colours, but black and white, and black and tan, also occur. The ideal height is 37cm (14in). The Sheltie's coat should keep it dry in any weather.

## OLD ENGLISH SHEEPDOG
The Old English Sheepdog is a strong, compact, burly dog. In the past the breed was used to herd cattle and sheep. The modern dog is only kept as a companion animal, a good example being even-tempered and hardy. It requires a fair amount of exercise and has a characteristic ambling gait at slow speeds and a remarkably elastic gallop. The abundant coat should be of a good hard texture and needs daily grooming down to the skin to prevent mats forming. The body colour can be any shade of blue-grey, set off by the white markings on the head, chest and front legs. This breed is always docked. The standard calls for a minimum size of 61cm (24in), but most animals are much larger.

## BEARDED COLLIE
The Bearded Collie, one of the native breeds of Scotland, is a long, lean, active dog, full of boisterous good humour. As well as being a sheepdog, it was also used for cattle droving, a role which ended with the advent of road and rail transport. It is now kept as a pet and a show dog. The shaggy coat is double and can be any shade of grey and brown, with or without white collie markings. The ideal height for this breed is 56cm (22in).

## BORDER COLLIE

The Border Collie is one of the finest working sheepdogs in the world, outstanding at controlling sheep at close quarters. It has been illustrated from medieval times, yet it was only in the late 19th century, with the development of sheepdog trials, that it got its present name. The early trial winners came from the Border country between Scotland and England. Being such keen workers, many Border Collies cannot relax into the more sedentary role of a pet. Frustrated with inactivity, they can become neurotic. The standard requires a height of 53cm (21in). The coat is usually black and white and may be either moderately long or smooth, but the hair should be short on the face and legs.

## ROUGH COLLIE

Originally a working dog, the Rough Collie is now kept as a pet and is also one of the most eye-catching show dogs. Selective breeding improved the size, coat and colouring of the original stock and added an elegance to the breed. It was one of the first breeds to enjoy a boom, with very high prices being paid for some specimens at the beginning of this century. The dog's chief glory is its dense, harsh, abundant outer coat. Three colours are accepted everywhere: sable, tricolour and blue merle, all usually marked with white. The all-white Rough Collie is recognized in the US alone. The height should be about 61cm (24in) and the weight about 29kg (65lb).

## SMOOTH COLLIE

The Smooth Collie should resemble the Rough Collie in all ways except its coat. Both types used to appear in the same litter and the Smooth was used as a working dog. However, the Rough Collie stole the limelight, leaving the Smooth in its shadows. The coat is short and flat with a harsh texture and the undercoat is very dense. The colour varieties are sable, tricolour and blue merle with typical white collie markings. Height and weight are the same as the Rough. Both dogs should have the same sweet, kindly expression, obtained by a combination and balance of skull shape, placement and colour of the eyes, and position and carriage of the ears.

## PEMBROKE WELSH CORGI

Of the two distinct breeds of corgi found in Wales, the Pembroke Welsh Corgi is by far the most popular, though there is no particular reason for this. Corgis belong to a family of cattle dogs colloquially known as 'heelers'. These are short-legged, noisy, active dogs whose job was to keep cattle on the move by nipping the heels of the laggards. Being small and agile, such dogs were able to dodge the flying hooves of the bullocks or ponies they were driving. The Pembroke is sturdy and tough, with a short, smooth, weather-resistant coat. This is nearly always some shade of red, though some small white markings are permissible. The foxy head has a wide, flat skull with pointed, erect ears. The short legs make the body look longer than it is. The tail is always docked. The maximum height is 30.5cm (12in) and the suggested weight 12kg (26.5lb), but most Corgis are heavier.

## CARDIGAN WELSH CORGI

There is a traditional belief that both Cardigan and Pembroke Corgis are very old Welsh breeds, although this is not supported by documentary evidence. However, both branches of the Corgi family must share a common root. The Cardigan has also the short legs and sturdy body of a cattle-heeling dog. It is even tempered, placid and easily trained. The most marked difference between the two breeds is that the Cardigan has a long tail. Traditionally, the dog should measure 91.5cm (36in) from tip of nose to tip of tail. It is the same height as the Pembroke but slightly heavier. The variety of colours is much greater, with shades of red and tricolours, dark brindle and white, or, most strikingly, blue merle.

Border Collie

Smooth Collie

Rough Collie

Cardigan Welsh Corgi

Pembroke Welsh Corgi

**Picardy Sheepdog**

**Beauceron**

**Pyrenean Sheepdog**

**Bouvier des Flandres**

**Briard**

## PICARDY SHEEPDOG

Of Europe's shaggy sheepdogs, the Picardy Sheepdog is believed to be one of the oldest. This is a dog from northern France, where it has been a guard and herding dog since the 9th century. A powerful, rugged animal, it stands 66cm (26in) tall. The ears are naturally erect. The long tail is carried low when the dog is standing and extended when it is moving. The shaggy, harsh coat is usually grey or fawn with lighter or darker shading.

## BEAUCERON

France's wide variety of shepherding breeds includes the Beauceron. This is a large, up-standing dog, usually with cropped ears and a long tail. It also has double hind dewclaws, a peculiarity of a number of French breeds. The coat is short, dense and harsh, usually black and tan, although grey, with or without black patches, is also as acceptable. The dog has strong guarding and herding instincts and is said to be easily trained. The height should be 70cm (27in).

## PYRENEAN SHEEPDOG

The Pyrenean Sheepdog is one of the smallest of the shaggy sheepdogs. It is also one of the most active, being full of nervous energy. Whereas the Pyrenean Mountain Dog was bred to guard the flocks, the Pyrenean Sheepdog was used to move them. A very eager and alert animal, the dog is reputed to be easily trained. A typical specimen is 51cm (20in) high and has a shaggy coat with a goat-like texture. Fawn, grey and brindle are the commonest shades.

## BOUVIER DES FLANDRES

The Bouvier des Flandres is one of the most popular breeds in Europe and is beginning to be shown in many other parts of the world. Originally it was used by the cattle-drovers of Flanders and parts of northern France. It is a big burly animal, heavy-boned and square in shape. Its vitality, constitution and size have made it ideal for police and army work. The expression is formed by the pronounced beard, moustache and eyebrows. The shaggy coat is dark grey or brindle. The Bouvier can be up to 68cm (27in) high, and weighs 40kg (88lb).

## BRIARD

The Briard, from the Province of Brie, is the best known of the French Sheepdogs. An active, racy animal, it needs plenty of exercise. During World War I it was trained for Red Cross work and also used to carry supplies to the troops. The Briard is a supple, muscular dog with an easy-going temperament. The long and wavy coat needs a lot of grooming. Plain, dark colours are preferred, though fawn with dark points is very common and popular. Double dewclaws on the hindlegs are considered to be very important. The height is 68cm (27in).

**Tibetan Terrier**

**German Shepherd Dog**

**Bernese Mountain Dog**

**Australian Cattle Dog**

**Australian Kelpie**

## TIBETAN TERRIER
In the past the Tibetan Terrier guarded flocks of sheep and goats, and also acted as a watchdog for the camel caravans carrying trade goods across the Himalayas. The word 'terrier' is a misnomer as this dog has few terrier traits, being an amenable and affectionate animal. It is a good house dog, but not aggressive or pugnacious. The coat is long and shaggy, completely obscuring the eyes. Colours include white, golden, cream, smoke grey, black or particolour. The height should be 40.5cm (16in).

## GERMAN SHEPHERD DOG
The German Shepherd is the most versatile of working dogs. It is a relatively recent breed, having been developed by German fanciers about 100 years ago from a mixture of working sheepdogs. It is the most widely used of working dogs because, as well as being alert and agile, it can be trained more easily than any other breed. Dogs of the right temperament make excellent pets, although they respond badly to mishandling or boredom. The height should be about 62.5cm (25in). The dog has a short but double coat, the harsh outer coat being very dense and weather resistant, and such a good insulator that the animal can work in most climates. Colour is of little account, although white is barred, but most dogs are shaded sable or black with fawn or gold markings.

## BERNESE MOUNTAIN DOG
The Bernese Mountain Dog could also be classed in the mastiff group. It has been included here as a cattle and droving dog because for centuries these strong, active animals were used by Swiss farmers to pull carts carrying dairy products to market. There are four Swiss mountain dog breeds, although this is the only one known outside its homeland. It is a handsome dog with a coat that is slightly wavy, silky and long. Colour is jet black with rich tan markings, a snow-white chest and a white blaze on the head. The height is 70cm (27in).

## AUSTRALIAN CATTLE DOG
The Australian Cattle Dog is primarily a working animal, a dog of terrific stamina able to herd cattle in conditions of heat and drought. The basic stock was probably the blue merle Smooth Collie and the native Dingo. Over the last 150 years, ruthless culling of animals unable to work has produced a very tough dog. The coat is short and rough. There are two colour varieties: mottled blue (with or without black markings) and red-speckled. The height is about 51cm (20in) and the weight about 18kg (40lb). Although shown in Australia, the breed is rarely seen elsewhere.

## AUSTRALIAN KELPIE
The Kelpie is the most widely used of Australia's sheepdogs. It is a quick-moving, untiring animal, able to work in hot temperatures. Like all dogs bred largely for work, it has particularly good legs and feet. The Kelpie is fast-thinking and fast-reacting, with a strong guarding instinct, and is famed for its strength of 'eye' – a mesmeric stare which it uses to control sheep. The Kelpie is shown in Australia and also competes in the sheepdog trials there. The smooth coat can be black and tan, red, black or blue. The height is about 51cm (20in) and the weight about 13.5kg (30lb).

## KOMONDOR

Many shepherd's dogs were simply kept as guards, to fight off wolves, bears, other dogs and human thieves. Such animals had to have a strong guarding instinct and a natural suspicion of any unusual occurrence. They had to be large, strong, agile and courageous. One of the most imposing is the Hungarian Komondor. It stands 80cm (31½in) high on average and weighs 51kg (135lb). The remarkable coat has coarse, long hairs that cling together to give a corded look, although if neglected it will mat. It provides protection against heat and cold, and also the teeth and claws of any opponents.

## HUNGARIAN PULI

The herding dog of the Hungarian plains is the Puli. Both this dog and the Komondor are believed to have originated with the Magyar tribes of the eastern Urals who migrated west to reach the Hungarian plains at the end of the 9th century. It is an agile and lively dog. Like the Komondor, the Puli has a coat which cords; in the adult animal it can look like voluminous skirts. The commonest colour is black, often dull and weathered-looking. The dog is 44.5cm (17½in) high and weighs 15kg (33lb).

## ROTTWEILER

The black and tan Rottweiler is used for police and guard work. The dog should be a picture of strength and agility combined with substance. It needs and responds well to careful training. The breed is named after the town of Rottweil in Germany, where from the Middle Ages it was used for droving, and often carried the cattle dealer's takings in a purse around its neck. With the end of droving, the Rottweiler declined drastically in numbers. Interest revived with its use by the German army at the beginning of this century. The dog stands 69cm (27in) high.

## GROENENDAEL

The Groenendael is the best known of four closely related Belgian Sheepdog breeds. It is graceful and well proportioned. It should appear robust without being heavily built. The coat, always black, should be long, straight and abundant, with a medium harsh texture. Used for many years by the Belgian Police, it has adapted well to the role of companion animal and family pet. All the Belgian Sheepdogs should be 66cm (26in) high.

## MALINOIS

The Malinois is a medium-sized dog with the high head carriage of all the Belgian Sheepdogs. Though now little used as a sheepdog, it has great potential as a guard dog, being wary yet not nervous. The coat is short, dense and coarse, with a wool undercoat. The colour includes all shades of red and fawn with a black overlay. The face should have a black mask.

Hungarian Puli

Komondor

Rottweiler

Malinois

Groenendael

**Tervueren**

**Laekenois**

**Canaan Dog**

**Maremma**

**Swedish Vallhund**

## TERVUEREN

The Tervueren, named after the town of Tervuren in Belgium, is similar in type, shape and colour to the Malinois, but has the long and abundant coat of the Groenendael. First bred in the 1890s, it was little known outside Belgium for the next 50 years. It is now gaining some popularity in the US for its prowess in obedience competitions.

## LAEKENOIS

The fourth Belgian Sheepdog is the Laekenois. Again, coat is the differentiating feature, this dog's being rough, dry and untidy looking. The hair should be about 6cm (2½in) long. The Belgian Sheepdogs, the French Beauceron, the German Shepherd and the Dutch herding breed all have similarities which suggest a common rootstock.

## MAREMMA

The Maremma, a large, strongly built guard dog from Italy, is thought to date back to Roman times and is still used as a working dog in its homeland. The coat is long and plentiful and rather harsh. The minimum height is 65cm (25½in). This is another all-white breed and it is thought that this colour was preferred as it enabled the shepherd to distinguish the dog quickly from predators.

## OWCZAREK NIZINNY

The Polish Lowland Sheepdog, the Owczarek Nizinny, is one of the smaller of the European shaggy sheepdogs, being under 52cm (20in). It is said to do well on very little food and to have an excellent memory. The coat can be straight or slightly wavy. There is no tail. All colours or combinations are acceptable. The Owczarek Nizinny makes a good companion animal.

## SWEDISH VALLHUND

The Swedish Vallhund is a cattle dog dating back over 1,000 years. There is a belief that Viking invaders took it to Wales but this has not been proven. The breed suffered near-extinction in this century but was saved by some well-timed publicity. It is 35cm high (13½in) and weighs 16kg (35lb). The Swedish Vallhund is usually greyish-brown or greyish yellow, shading to a lighter colour on the lower parts of the body.

**Owczarek Nizinny**

## CANAAN DOG

Recognized as the native breed of Israel, the Canaan Dog has been little seen elsewhere except the US. It has been used as a watchdog for herds and flocks and also makes a very good guard. Up to 61cm (24in) in height, it weighs about 25kg (55lb). The coat should be medium-long, straight and coarse. The plumed tail is carried over the back. Colours include sandy, reddish-brown, white and black.

# TOY DOGS

Toy dogs have existed and been admired for as long as there have been written records. Indeed among the remains of prehistoric dogs, typical dwarf forms have been found, and many visual records exist of their development through the ages – they appear on scrolls and ceramics, in tapestries and in paintings. Toy dogs can be seen in many of the portraits commissioned by their rich and aristocratic owners so that the progress of dwarf spaniels, small greyhounds and tiny terriers can be traced down the centuries. Most toy dogs have a great deal of personality and therein lies much of their charm. Though existing only to amuse and befriend, many are as active and energetic as their larger prototypes and, treated sensibly, are as hardy and intelligent as most other companion breeds.

### CAVALIER KING CHARLES SPANIEL
The Cavalier King Charles and the King Charles Spaniels take their name from their 17th century ancestors who were so favoured by Charles II of England. Of the two dogs, the Cavalier is much closer to the original type as drawn by artists such as Reynolds. It is a well balanced and sensible dog. One of the larger toys, it weighs about 8kg (18lb). The four colour varieties are the same as in the King Charles.

**Cavalier King Charles**

### KING CHARLES SPANIEL
From the same root-stock as the Cavalier, the King Charles Spaniel has been greatly modified to have a well-rounded head and a turned-up nose, giving a very aristocratic expression. The weight is 6.5kg (14lb). The toy spaniel breeds have four distinct colour varieties. These are: the Blenheim (pearly white with well distributed chestnut-red patches); the Tricolour (pearly white with black patches and brilliant tan markings); the Black and Tan (glossy jet black with mahogany markings); and the Ruby (rich red).

**King Charles Spaniel**

### GRIFFON BRUXELLOIS
Resembling a comical urchin, the Griffon Bruxellois is descended from a Belgian ratting dog, which was crossed with the German Affenpinscher, also with the Pug. Griffons vary in size but 4kg (9lb) is average. The harsh, wiry coat needs much trimming if the dog is to look at its best. Colours are red, black, and black and tan.

**Griffon Bruxellois**

### YORKSHIRE TERRIER
Once much larger, the Yorkshire Terrier was kept by Yorkshire miners as a ratter. Over the years the size was reduced and the coat lengthened. Today some are as small as 1.1kg (2½lb) though the standard specifies up to 3.1kg (7lb). The lustrous hair should be straight and floor-length, with long whiskers, beard and head hair. The topknot is tied with ribbon. The colour should be a dark steel blue on the body with tan markings on the face, legs and feet.

**Yorkshire Terrier**

**Italian Greyhound**

33cm (13in) high and weighing 4kg (9lb). The coat is long, soft and wavy and can be any colour or particolour. Affectionate and happy, the Lowchen makes a good companion.

### PAPILLON
The French Papillon's ears are meant to resemble butterfly wings – hence the name. Ideally, the forehead should

**Bichon Frise**

have a white blaze to suggest the insect's body. Different countries set different sizes but 28cm (11in) is about the maximum. The ears should be heavily fringed and the tail plumed over the back. There should be a profuse frill on the chest and also on the back of the thighs. Most Papillons are white, patched with another colour, usually red or black.

**Papillon**

### ITALIAN GREYHOUND
The Italian Greyhound has been valued as a ladies' pet and a companion to the fashionable for nearly 3,000 years. Like all toy dogs, it loves fuss and attention from people it knows. With so little protection against the cold and wet, it needs a lot of care. Colours include all shades of fawn, cream, blue and pied. It weighs about 3.5kg (8lb).

### BICHON FRISE
Small white dogs with flowing coats have been long admired, their portraits appearing in many European paintings from the 16th century on. The French Bichon Frise gets its name from its soft, corkscrew curls. The height should be under 28cm (11in). The coat should measure 7–10cm (2¼–4in). When shown in Europe the dog's coat is shaggy and curled; in the US and the UK it is scissored to give a rounded appearance.

### MALTESE
The Maltese is invariably white, though it may have slight lemon markings. It was thought to have originated on Malta, from where it was taken along the trade routes of the ancient world. It should not be over 25.5cm (10in) or weigh over 2.5kg (6lb). If the Maltese is to be shown, the coat requires much attention.

### LOWCHEN
The Lowchen has the nickname 'Little Lion Dog' as it is shaved to have a mane, and a plume on the tail. It is one of the larger toy dogs, being about

**Maltese**

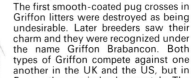

### GRIFFON BRABANCON
The first smooth-coated pug crosses in Griffon litters were destroyed as being undesirable. Later breeders saw their charm and they were recognized under the name Griffon Brabancon. Both types of Griffon compete against one another in the UK and the US, but in Europe they are judged separately. The Brabancon's coat should be smooth and dense and the colours similar to those of the Bruxellois. Both kinds of Griffon are among the most intelligent and determined of small dogs.

### ENGLISH TOY TERRIER
The English Toy Terrier (the 'Toy Manchester' in the US) is a smooth-coated black and tan dog, once much esteemed as a vermin killer. About 150 years ago similar dogs were matched against each other in ratting contests. Size varies but the ideal weight is 3.5kg (8lb) and the height 30.5cm (12in). The coat should be short, thick and glossy. They are affectionate and make excellent house dogs.

**Griffon Brabancon**

**English Toy Terrier**

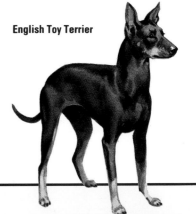

**Lowchen**

Long Coat Chihuahua

Smooth Coat Chihuahua

Toy Fox Terrier

Affenpinscher

Pekingese

Japanese Spaniel

## LONG COAT CHIHUAHUA

The two breeds of Chihuahua are distinguished only by their coats. Both types may appear in the same litter. The breeds contain the smallest dogs in the world, but smallness should not mean lack of quality and soundness. The preferred weight is 1–1.5kg (2–4lb). Any colour is permissible. The long coat should be thick and soft, lying flat on the body. There is feathering on the feet and legs, a ruff on the neck and a plumed tail.

## SMOOTH COAT CHIHUAHUA

The Smooth Coat Chihuahua was for a long time the most popular of the two breeds. The dog was named after the Mexican state where it was discovered by North American visitors in the 1850s. It is a neat, alert dog with a saucy expression. Though suspicious of strange people, it is perfectly prepared to hold its own against other dogs. This bravura, combined with its agility, accounts for much of its success as a show and companion dog.

## TOY FOX TERRIER

The Toy Fox Terrier in the US, like the Jack Russell Terrier in the UK, is one of the breeds that, though much bred, is not recognized by any Kennel Club so cannot be shown. Most influential of the small breeds used in the attempt to create a tiny, smooth Fox Terrier has been the Chihuahua, as shown by the large erect ear. The tail is docked. The dog is white with black or tan markings and weighs about 3kg (6.5lb).

## AFFENPINSCHER

The Affenpinscher – meaning 'monkey terrier' – comes from Germany. It can be traced back to the 16th century, to a rough haired version of the Miniature Pinscher. Since then the nose has been shortened to give the monkey-like expression. The Affenpinscher is a hardy dog, with an expression which mixes comical self-importance and zealous loyalty. It is devoted to those it knows, but uninterested in the casual stranger. The dog should be 28cm (11in) in height and weigh about 4kg (9lb). The coat is wiry and black.

## JAPANESE SPANIEL

The Japanese Spaniel, known as the Japanese Chin in the UK, is one of a group of snub-nosed dogs from the Orient. Once a favourite of the Japanese Imperial family, it reached the West in the mid 19th century, where it was briefly popular until the Pekingese stole the spotlight. An alert dog, its eye-whites give it a look of astonishment. The profuse coat is soft and silky to touch. The colour is white, patched with red or black. The dog should not exceed 3kg (7lb).

## PEKINGESE

Kept for many centuries exclusively at the court of the Chinese Emperors, the Pekingese reached the West after British troops sacked the Imperial Palace at Peking in 1860. The Peke combines determination with an aura of unhurried dignity. With weak owners it can become spoilt, but treated sensibly it is an animal of charm and intelligence. The great wealth of coat can be any colour. The dog should not weigh more than 5kg (11lb).

## CHINESE CRESTED DOG

Hairless dogs are rare, and little is known of their origins. The Chinese Crested Dog has no proven link with China but the 'crested' refers to the fine plume on the head. Apart from this, and some leg and tail fur, the dog is hairless. Not having the insulation of a coat, it needs care to avoid sunburn, chills and draughts. Colours can include grey, bronze, pink, lilac or blue. It should weigh 3–5.5kg (7–12lb).

Chinese Crested Dog

## MINIATURE PINSCHER

The Miniature Pinscher is one of the smartest of the toy breeds. It is a spirited dog, alert to every sound and rarely still. It makes a good family dog. The height should be about 30cm (12in). The smooth coat is usually a solid red, though black and tan, blue and tan, or chocolate and tan are also accepted in some countries. The dog's high-stepping action adds to its showy appeal.

## PUG

The heavyweight of the toy group, the Pug can weigh up to 8kg (18lb). It has one of the most tightly curled tails of all dogs. The short, smooth coat merely needs polishing with a chamois leather. The Pug probably originated in China and was discovered by Dutch merchants. It was brought to the UK when William of Orange took the throne in 1689, and became extremely fashionable during the 18th and 19th centuries. The colour can be fawn or black.

## SHIH TZU

The importance of the lion in Buddhist legend led to the creation of several types of 'Lion Dogs' to serve as symbols. One such, the Shih Tzu, originated in Tibet, and is associated with the monasteries where it is esteemed for its religious significance. It is an active, independent dog. The coat is long and dense and can be any colour. The Shih Tzu should not be more than 26.5cm (10½in) high and can weigh up to 7.5 kg (16lb).

## LHASA APSO

Admirers of the Lhasa Apso do not regard it as a toy dog. However, with an ideal height of 25.5cm (10in) it is one of the smaller breeds. This is another one of the four Tibetan breeds recognized in the West. Lhasa Apsos were kept mainly as watchdogs in Tibet. They are still wary of strangers but are lively and playful with those they know. The Lhasa Apso can be almost any shade but golden and honey colours are preferred.

## POMERANIAN

The Pomeranian is the tiniest version of the spitz. A vivacious and self-important animal, it makes an alert if noisy watchdog. Early Pomeranians weighed as much as 13.5kg (30lb). They

**Miniature Pinscher**

**Shih Tzu**

**Pug**

**Australian Silky Terrier**

**Tibetan Spaniel**

**Lhasa Apso**

**Pomeranian**

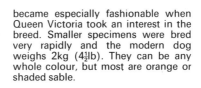

could be related to the Pekinese. There is a story that Tibetan Spaniels were used to turn the Buddhist prayer wheels. It is a hardy dog and a good companion for country as well as town dwellers. It can be any colour, though most are fawn. The height should be about 25.5cm (10in) and the weight can be as much as 6.5kg (15lb).

became especially fashionable when Queen Victoria took an interest in the breed. Smaller specimens were bred very rapidly and the modern dog weighs 2kg (4½lb). They can be any whole colour, but most are orange or shaded sable.

## TIBETAN SPANIEL

The origins of the Tibetan Spaniel are speculative, though it looks as if it

## AUSTRALIAN SILKY TERRIER

The Australian Silky Terrier was created about 80 years ago in Sydney from a mixture of small terriers, the most influential being the Yorkshire. It is alert, keen and full of vigour. The coat is very important, being fine, glossy and silky. It should be about 15cm (6in) long and a rich, dark blue and tan in colour. The dog is approximately 23cm (9in) high and weighs about 4kg (10lb).

# MISCELLANEOUS GROUP

The obscure origins and history of some breeds means that they cannot be put into any category. Each Kennel Club has a different way of classifying these breeds – for example, the English Club calls them Utility dogs, while the American Club calls them Non-sporting dogs. The breeds in this miscellaneous group have been put here either because their original function is so different from their modern role that they could not be grouped elsewhere, or because their origins are so vague that their relationships to other breeds is unclear.

**Dobermann**

**Giant Schnauzer**

**Standard Schnauzer**

**Miniature Schnauzer**

## DOBERMANN

In the 1880s, Herr Dobermann, a German tax collector, created the dog which bears his name. Like many pioneer breeders, he was reticent about the breeds he used to create this guard dog, but one was probably the existing German Pinscher. The early dogs had very suspicious characters, making them ideal for police and army work. Over the years they have been made less volatile. Today, they are one of the most alert breeds. Colour is usually black and tan, but brown and tan and blue and tan are accepted. Some countries recognize the parchment shade, Isabella. The ideal height is 68.5cm (27in).

## SCHNAUZERS

'Schnauzer' means muzzle. This feature of the breed is accentuated by its wiry beard and whiskers, a look which requires expert trimming to achieve. Schnauzers were used as general-purpose farm dogs, guarding, hunting or herding as the need arose. The **Standard Schnauzer** is a breed with a well-documented history going back at least four centuries. It is a robust, muscular dog, which should be stable and confident in temperament with a tough and hardy constitution. The coat is weather resistant, with a harsh wiry top coat over a dense undercoat. Colour can be black or any shade of pepper and salt (a mixture of light and dark grey hairs). The height is about 48cm (19in). The **Giant Schnauzer**, the least common of the Schnauzers, was used as a droving dog and would have died out when this ended had it not been realized that its size, hardiness and intelligence made it ideal for police and army work and it is widely used in Europe as a security dog and frontier guard. The height is about 70cm (27in). The colour is usually black. Both the Standard and the Giant are slow-maturing dogs with a corresponding longevity. The **Miniature Schnauzer** is the youngest of the three Schnauzers and also the most popular worldwide. It is among the top ten breeds in the US. It was reduced in size from the Standard, to 35.5cm (14in), by crosses with the Affenpinscher. It is easily trained.

Dalmatian

a hardy animal, said to be aggressive with other dogs. There are two coat varieties – long and curly coated – and the hindquarters are usually shaved with a plume being left on the end of the long tail. Colours include black, brown or dark grey, all of which may be marked with white. The height is about 57cm (22in).

## PINSCHER
A much older breed than the Dobermann, the German Pinscher has remained relatively unknown compared with its larger cousin or its smaller relative, the Miniature Pinscher. It is a smooth-coated, medium-sized dog, which makes a lively and alert companion. The eyes are dark and sparkling and the glossy coat is usually black and tan or deep red. The height is about 48cm (19in).

## DALMATIAN
Dalmatians appear in many 17th-century paintings, in settings that suggest it was used as a hunting dog. Later it became fashionable to have one running under or behind one's horse-drawn carriage. The coat should appear sleek and glossy. The ground colour is always pure white but the spots, unique in the canine world, can be either black or liver. They should measure 1–2.5cm ($\frac{1}{2}$–1in). The maximum height is 61cm (24in) and the weight about 25kg (55lb).

## PORTUGESE WATER DOG
The Portugese Water Dog was once used by fishermen to retrieve tackle from the sea, act as ship-to-shore messengers and guard the boat in port. It is

## POODLES
The name 'poodle' comes from the German 'pudel', meaning to splash in water. The oldest breed, the **Standard Poodle**, is also the biggest, with a minimum height of 38cm (15in). The profuse coat makes all three breeds look bigger than they really are. The poodle was orginally used in Europe as a sporting dog, its fondness for water making it an asset to hunters of water fowl. The dog is accepted in a wide range of solid colours, including brown, black, white, cream, silver, blue. Particoloured dogs are not accepted. The **Miniature Poodle** must be under 38cm (15in) in height but should resemble the Standard, from which it was developed, in all other ways. It first became popular at the end of the 19th century. Clipping the coat is very important with the poodle breeds, the continental or lion clip being essential for the adult show poodle. Pets can be given more manageable coats. Poodles do not moult but frequent grooming is needed to prevent mats forming. The **Toy Poodle** is the youngest of the three breeds and rose to fame in the 1950s. The height definitions of poodle breeds vary from country to country. In the UK, Toy Poodles must be under 28cm (11in), in the US under 25cm (10in), while in Europe they can be up to 35.5cm (14in). The Toy has all the sparkle and showmanship of its larger relatives as well as the same basic shape. It should be an active, elegant dog, carrying itself with pride, qualities that have made it one of today's most popular breeds.

Portuguese Water Dog

Pinscher

Standard Poodle

Miniature Poodle

Toy Poodle

# GUNDOGS

The superior sense of smell of the dog has made it the most valued of man's hunting companions. With the invention of firearms, it was no longer enough for a dog to follow a scent then chase and bring to bay or pull down the game. Dogs were still required to find the prey and indicate its position by pointing or setting, but they then had to flush it out to be shot. As the range of the weapons improved, they were also expected to find and retrieve the shot birds. Today many gundogs are kept only as show dogs and companions.

**Labrador Retriever**

**Golden Retriever**

**Chesapeake Bay Retriever**

**Flat-coated Retriever**

## LABRADOR RETRIEVER
The Labrador is one of the best known and most widely kept of the retrieving breeds. Originally from Newfoundland, they were brought to the UK in the 1870s. Many still work in the field, but more are now kept as companions. The are also used as guide dogs and drug sniffing dogs. This versatility stems from the breed's cheerfulness and reliability, and its strength and stamina. The height should be about 57cm 22in). The dense, short coat is water resistant enabling the dog to retrieve wildfowl without getting chilled. The colour is generally either black or yellow, but chocolate, though unusual, is also acceptable.

## GOLDEN RETRIEVER
The Golden Retriever is a kind, sensible and good-natured dog, used for a number of roles including that of guide dog. It is also shown extensively. The coat can range from a deep glowing yellow through to cream. Retrievers are expected to work in water, swimming out to fetch shot birds, and the Golden is no exception. For this reason the coat is both dense and water resistant. The height is 61cm (24in) and the weight about 36kg (80lb).

## CHESAPEAKE BAY RETRIEVER
The Chesapeake Bay Retriever stems from two puppies which were rescued from a shipwreck off the coast of Maryland in the US. Found to be excellent retrievers, they were crossed with local sporting dogs to create a new retrieving breed. The bay after which they are named is a wildfowler's paradise. The height is about 66cm (26in) and the weight about 34kg (75lb). The outer coat is oily, making it waterproof, and the deadgrass colour, which varies from faded tan to dull straw, gives the dog camouflage.

## FLAT-COATED RETRIEVER
The Flat-Coated Retriever was most popular as a working dog during the 19th century, being a favourite of gamekeepers employed on the big estates. It now has only a modest following. Like all retrievers, it is strong with plenty of stamina. The weight should be about 35kg (80lb). Most are black in colour with a soft sheen to the hair.

## CURLY-COATED RETRIEVER

The Curly-Coated Retriever is probably the oldest of the retrieving breeds and was a very popular working gundog in the 19th century. It is the tallest of the retrievers, standing 68.5cm (27in) high. It weighs up to 36kg (80lb). It has a good nose and is very intelligent. Like all gundogs it needs plenty of exercise to keep it in good condition. Unlike some of this group, it makes a good guard dog. The distinctive coat suggests water spaniel origins. Though the muzzle and foreface are smooth, the rest of the dog is covered with a mass of crisp, small curls, down to the tip of the tail. It gives the dog an old-fashioned air, as if it has stepped straight from a sporting print of the past. The colour can be either black or liver.

**Curly-coated Retriever**

**English Setter**

**Gordon Setter**

**Irish Setter**

## ENGLISH SETTER

Netting wildfowl in medieval times was done with the help of dogs called 'setting spaniels'. They were expected to search for coveys of feeding birds, such as quail, and indicate their position by crouching motionless as soon as they scented game. From these dogs probably come both the present day setters and the spaniels. The English Setter is the oldest of the three setter breeds, having been in existence for at least 200 years. Most are kept today as show dogs and pets. It is a friendly, elegant and beautifully coloured animal, the long, slightly wavy coat being white flecked or mottled with black, lemon or orange markings. The height should be about 68.5cm (27in) and the weight about 30kg (66lb).

## GORDON SETTER

The Gordon Setter is the only gundog to have originated in Scotland. From the 1870s onwards the dukes of Gordon bred it for use on their grouse moors. The flat, silky coat is coal black in colour with chestnut-red tan markings. The Gordon is more heavily built that the other setter and about 66cm (26in) in height. The dog should be a tireless and willing worker, being both persistent and determined. However, few are used as gundogs today. The Gordon is a rather reserved and dignified dog, lacking the extrovert personality that makes an impact in the show ring. It a breed that has to be kept for its loyalty and intelligence to be appreciated.

## IRISH SETTER

The Irish Setter, often nicknamed the Red Setter, is a flamboyant dog with a coat of rich, chestnut red. The dark brown eyes have a kindly expression, giving the face a limpid look with a touch of mischief about it. It is a dog built on galloping lines, meant to quarter the ground ahead of the sportsman, with head held high to catch the airborne scent of a game bird. Few, however, are used for hunting today. Their high spirits and energy have ensured their popularity. A 100 or so years ago the breed was nearly all red and white. Today, the only white mark might be the occasional star on the chest. The modern dog is bigger, with heights of up to 68.5cm (27in) and weights around 31.5kg (70lb).

**Large Munsterlander**

**Small Munsterlander**

**Wetterhoun**

it is held in a spiral curled over the croup. The entire body except the head is covered with coarse, thick, curly hair which feels oily to the touch. The colours include all-black, or white with heavy brown or blue markings. The height is about 54.5cm (21in).

## POINTER

The Pointer is a large, active dog built on galloping lines and seen at its best working across open country. The heyday of the working Pointer was in the 19th century when large sporting estates were common. Today, it is used mainly in the US for its original job of finding game. The dog's development was dictated by improvements in the sporting gun. Early 18th-century, muzzle-loading guns took time to load and fire. A dog was needed which could find the game and indicate its position, remaining steady on point while the sportsman prepared to shoot. These first pointers were heavily built, slow-moving animals. As guns improved, greyhounds and foxhounds were used to add more speed. The short coat is mostly white with lemon, orange, liver or black markings. The height should be 68.5cm (27in).

## GERMAN SHORT-HAIRED POINTER

The German Short-Haired Pointer is one of the most widely used gundogs, popular in both Europe and the US. The original dog was heavy, and slow but had an excellent nose and a calm temperament. To add speed and style, German breeders crosssed it with the English Pointer. The dog does well at shows, but most breeders want to preserve its working ability by using it as a shooting companion and running it in field trials. The short coat is usually liver and white in a ticked or roan pattern, but solid liver or black are acceptable. The height can be up to 63.5cm (25in) and the weight up to 30kg (66lb).

end's shooting trip. It is a good-natured dog. The coat is fairly long, with feathering on the ears, legs and tail. The head is usually dark brown with small white markings and the body white with large brown patches and flecks. The height is about 53.5cm (21in) and the weight 16kg (35lb). The Small Munsterlander is one of a group of breeds which fall midway between the setters and the spaniels in looks.

## WETTERHOUN

The Wetterhoun is a water spaniel of Dutch origin and was once used to hunt otters. Now it is kept mainly as a house and guard dog as it has a strong sense of its own territory and the courage to defend it. It is a sturdily built dog with a short, thick body and neck, giving it a low head carriage. The tail carriage is a very distinctive feature for

## LARGE MUNSTERLANDER

Many European gundog breeds are expected not only to find and flush game but to retrieve it when it is shot. One such dog is the Large Munsterlander from Germany. It works equally well on land or in water. It is seen more often in the field than in the show ring, and its breeders are keen to preserve its working abilities. As with all retrievers, the teeth should meet in a perfect scissor bite. The coat should be long and dense, without any curl. The tail and legs are well feathered. The head is black with minimal white markings and the body is white with black patches and flecks. The height of the male dog is about 61cm (24in) and the weight about 29.5kg (65lb).

## SMALL MUNSTERLANDER

The Small Munsterlander, also from Germany, is one of the smallest of the all-purpose gundogs. For this reason it is kept by town dwellers who want a dog which can fit in with urban life, whilst being able to take on a week-

**Pointer**

**German Short-haired Pointer**

## WEIMARANER

The Weimaraner has been nicknamed the 'ghost dog' for its colour is always grey. Silver grey is preferred, though shades of mouse or roe grey are acceptable. It has a metallic sheen and this and its pale amber or blue-grey eyes make it a distinctive breed. First bred in the town of Weimar, Germany, by a group of aristocratic sportsmen, ownership of the breed was jealously guarded for over a century. It was not until after World War I that some dogs reached the US, where their all-round ability made them popular among field trial enthusiasts and other sportsmen. The dog was first used to track deer and boar and only later to find, point, flush and retrieve game birds. It has also been used as a police dog. The height is about 68.5cm (27in).

## GERMAN WIRE-HAIRED POINTER

The German Wire-haired Pointer is less than a century old, yet has become one of the most popular of working gundogs in Germany and surrounding countries. It was developed from the Pudlêpointer, a rough-haired dog fond of water, which was crossed with the smooth-coated pointers and the Airedale Terrier. The dog excels in hunting the bigger forest game. Tough in build and temperament, it makes a good guard dog. It can measure 67cm (26in) and can weigh up to 34kg (75lb). The harsh coat is often liver or liver and white ticked.

## BRACCO ITALIANO

The only short-haired pointing breed in Italy is the Bracco Italiano. It has an old-fashioned air and a distinctly hound-like head. It originally had two colour variations: the orange and white and the roan chestnut. It is a well-proportioned, powerful dog with a loose-limbed, heavily boned appearance. The head, carried high, should have a serious and kindly expression. It is a diligent, methodical dog, painstaking in its work of finding game, and docile in temperament. The height and weight are very variable, ranging from 54.5cm to 67cm (21in to 26in), and 25kg to 39.5kg (55lb to 88lb). The coat is glossy.

## HUNGARIAN VIZSLA

The most widely known of the Hungarian gundogs is the Vizsla. Game used to be plentiful on the plains of Hungary and the Vizsla was expected to find it with ease. The Vizsla was required to be a good tracking dog and work fairly close to the gun. It is affectionate, sensitive, and obedient, so can be easily trained. Though there is a wire-haired variety, the short-haired version, with its unique russet gold coat, is the one most often seen. The head is gaunt and noble with powerful jaws. The body is lean and muscular and the movement graceful. The height is about 63.5cm (25in) and the weight 30kg (66lb).

Weimaraner

German Wire-haired Pointer

Bracco Italiano

Hungarian Vizsla

## AMERICAN COCKER SPANIEL

A number of gundog breeds are rarely used for their original work but have become popular as pets and show dogs. The American Cocker Spaniel was the most popular dog in the US for 17 years (1936–52), longer than any other pedigree breed. The dog was developed from British spaniels. It is smaller than the English Cocker, with a shorter back, a sloping top line and a much longer neck. The greatest changes, though, can be seen in the American dog's domed skull, accentuated by the trimmed ears, and its long, silky coat, which reaches the ground. Colours include black, black and tan, buff and particolour. The ideal height is 38.75cm (15in).

American Cocker Spaniel

Clumber Spaniel

## CLUMBER SPANIEL

The heaviest of the spaniels is the Clumber, with an ideal weight of 36kg (80lb). The breed originated in France but was developed in England. At the time of the French Revolution, the Duc de Noailles presented some of his dogs to the Duke of Newcastle from whose estate, Clumber Park, they took their name. As a working dog the Clumber is quiet, persistent and slow. Though hefty enough to force its way through thick cover, its lack of speed is considered a major drawback. The dog has a characteristic rolling gait due to a broad, long body being set on short, strong legs. The dense coat is silky and straight. The coat should be white in colour with slight lemon markings on the head and muzzle.

## BRITTANY SPANIEL

As a working gundog, the Brittany Spaniel has made a great impression both in Europe and the US in the last 50 years, having all-round abilities as a utility gundog and a field trial competitor. At first glance the Brittany resembles a robust setter in build, albeit with a tail docked short. It is fast, strong and enthusiastic. Originally used to point and flush woodcock, the Brittany adapted easily to finding other types of game birds, such as the American bobwhite quail. The coat is flat and fine. The dog is mainly white with orange or red patches. Black and white or tricolour is also accepted. The height is 50cm (20in) and the weight is about 15kg (33lb).

## COCKER SPANIEL

The Cocker Spaniel is the most popular of the spaniel breeds in the UK, due in great part to its merry and affectionate character. A typical Cocker should have a tail that never stops wagging and a soulful, melting expression. It is kept almost entirely as a pet and is rarely used in the field. The coat is silky and flat and needs grooming and trimming to keep it in order. One of the attractions of the Cocker is the wide range of colours that is found in the breed. Solid colours include black, red and golden, but particolours, roans and black and tans are also acceptable. The Cocker Spaniel should be about 40.5cm (16in) in height and weigh about 14.5kg (32lb).

Brittany Spaniel

Cocker Spaniel

**English Springer Spaniel**

**Irish Water Spaniel**

**Welsh Springer Spaniel**

### IRISH WATER SPANIEL
The earliest division of the spaniels was between the land spaniels and the water spaniels. From the latter are descended only the Irish Water Spaniel and the American Water Spaniel. The Irish dog began to be bred as a type from 1850 onwards, being ideal for the salt marshes and estuaries where water fowl lived. This is a powerfully-built animal with a great enthusiasm for its work. It is unlike any other spaniel, being much larger and having a closely curled coat of liver puce ringlets. The face is smooth with a curly topknot. The full length tail is also unique, having curls which stop abruptly to leave the rest of the tail bare. The coat is oily and therefore strong smelling. The height is about 58.5cm (23in).

### ENGLISH SPRINGER SPANIEL
As in a number of gundog breeds, the show type and the working type of the English Springer Spaniel are quite distinct. The working dog is both smaller and more energetic than the show dog. Before the advent of the gun, spaniels were used to flush or 'spring' birds into nets or for waiting falcons or greyhounds. This is a big spaniel, being about 51cm (20in) high and some 22.5kg (50lb) in weight. The coat is close and water resistant. Most English Springers are liver and white, but black and white and tricolour are also acceptable.

### WELSH SPRINGER SPANIEL
The Welsh Springer Spaniel and the Brittany Spaniel probably share the same Celtic root. Certainly, the Welsh Springer is a very old spaniel breed with a likeness both in form and colour that can be traced in portraits from the 1700s onwards. It has always been valued in Wales as a tireless hunter, able to work in the harsh climate and rough terrain of the Welsh hills. During this century, it has had some success in the show ring, due in part to its pearly white colouring splashed with deep, rich red. The height should not exceed 48cm (19in).

### SUSSEX SPANIEL
The Sussex Spaniel has been known in the English county from which it takes its name for nearly 200 years. It should be about 40.5cm (16in) in height and weigh about 20.5kg (45lb), although many dogs are larger. The head is wide with frowning brows over soft, expressive, hazel eyes. An active breed, it needs plenty of exercise. The striking coat should be a rich, golden colour, with a glistening sheen, an effect produced by golden tips on the hairs. The Sussex was bred to force game from bramble and gorse, and it gives tongue while doing so. Modern sportsmen prefer a silent dog so it is rarely worked with the gun now.

### FIELD SPANIEL
Field and Cocker Spanies spring from the same taproot and were not separated into different breeds until 1892. The Field Spaniel is a slightly larger dog, being about 46cm (18in) in height and weighing 25kg (55lb). It is a self-coloured dog, usually black or liver. Its expression is rather grave, that of a level-headed, reliable dog that is docile and affectionate. Numbers in this breed have always been somewhat low, perhaps because of the sombre colouring and lack of sparkle compared with the Cocker.

**Sussex Spaniel**

**Field Spaniel**

# MASTIFF AND BULL BREEDS

The mastiff group contains many of the heaviest dogs. Such massive and courageous animals have always been prized as dogs of war, guardians of their owner's possessions, and as hunting dogs prepared to bring to bay big game. Assyrian murals dating from about 700BC show mastiffs going out to hunt lions with the Assyrian kings. Courage and a disregard for pain were the qualities which gave mastiffs their renown and from them are also descended the fighting and bull-baiting breeds which, from the time of the Roman circuses until animal baiting was outlawed in the 19th century, provided spectators with such cruel 'sport'.

Great Dane

Bullmastiff

Boxer

Mastiff

### GREAT DANE
One of the most popular of the giant breeds, the Great Dane is Germanic and not Danish in origin. The dog was kept by the German nobility as a companion and guard. It was also used to hunt boars. Owners must have the space and money to provide for a dog which stands a minimum of 76cm (30in) and weighs about 54kg (120lb). It is usually gentle with friends and tolerant of children. Except in the UK, the ears are generally cropped. Fawn with a dark mask is the usual colour, but brindle, black and blue are acceptable. The coat of the rare Harlequin Dane is spectacular, being pure white with a scattering of black patches.

### BULLMASTIFF
The Bullmastiff was developed in the 19th century by crossing the ponderous Mastiff with a lighter, more active Bulldog. The resulting dog was powerful but not too cumbersome. A 100 years ago, this breed accompanied gamekeepers, who valued a dark silent dog on their nightly patrols against poachers. Once the poachers had been surprised, the dog was strong and active enough to overtake and knock down a fleeing man. Red and fawn are the most popular colours. Males can be up to 68.5cm (27in) and weigh 58.5kg (130lb).

### BOXER
The Boxer was created about 90 years ago in Germany. Neither the reason for the name nor the original stock are known for certain, although the Bulldog was involved. The Boxer was used for guard and security work in its homeland but was little known outside until after World War II. It is good natured and full of boisterous energy. A black mask is essential and the ears are cropped where this is still legal. The coat is usually fawn or brindle with white markings. The height is 63cm (25in) and the weight 32kg (70lb).

### MASTIFF
The Mastiff breed has been known in the UK since pre-Roman times. Impressed by the dog's ferocity and size, the invading Romans sent a number back to Rome to fight lions, men and each other in the amphitheatres. The modern dog should combine grandeur, good nature, courage and docility. The taller and heavier it is the better, provided proportion and balance are not sacrificed. The minimum height for a dog is 76cm (30in). Colours include apricot, fawn and fawn brindle. The muzzle, ears and nose should be black.

**Newfoundland**

**Hovawart**

**Leonberger**

**Pyrenean Mountain Dog**

**St Bernard**

## NEWFOUNDLAND
The forerunners of this breed were used by fishermen of Labrador and Newfoundland to retrieve gear from the water, haul in nets and carry lines to shore. They have also been used as lifeguards on French beaches because they can survive in very rough seas. The coat is oily and may be either dull jet black or bronze, both of which may have small white markings on the chest and feet. The third colour variety is the black and white Landseer. The optimum size is 71cm (28in) and the weight 69kg (150lb).

## HOVAWART
The Hovawart, meaning 'farm watchdog', is an attempt to recreate a dog known in Germany in medieval times, by a careful mixture of the farm dogs from the more mountainous and isolated areas of Germany. A general utility dog, it is used to guard property, fetch in the cattle, and accompany its owner rough-shooting. The height is about 70cm (27in) and the weight up to 40kg (88lb). Many are deep golden, or black with some white hairs at the tail tip.

## LEONBERGER
The Leonberger, named after the German town of Leonberg, was reputedly produced from crosses between the St Bernard and the Newfoundland, in an attempt to create a dog resembling the lions on the town's coat of arms. Leonbergers are now mainly tawny in colour with a thick, fairly long coat, free from waves and curls. In the past, it has been used as a draught dog and for protecting farm stock. The height is about 80cm (32in).

## PYRENEAN MOUNTAIN DOG
French Shepherds once used the Pyrenean Mountain Dog to protect their flocks against attack from wolves. The breed first became fashionable with the French nobility in the 18th century, who found such dogs both ornamental and useful in guarding their chateaux. The thick, double coat is white, often with markings of badger, grey or tan. The dog has double dewclaws on each hindleg. Great size is essential, with the minimum height being 71cm (28in) and the minimum weight 49.5kg (110lb).

## ST BERNARD
The St Bernard was first used by the monks of the Hospice of St Bernard in the Swiss Alps in the 17th century. Although they performed several tasks, they are best known for their work as guide dogs, and their ability to find lost travellers in the mountains. Most modern dogs are rough-coated with fairly long, flat hair. The minimum size is 70cm (27.5in). Colours include orange and mahogany-brindle, with white markings and black shadings on the face and ears.

Bulldog

Neapolitan Mastiff

Dogue de Bordeaux

French Bulldog

Boston Terrier

## NEAPOLITAN MASTIFF

An impressive mastiff from Italy, the Neapolitan Mastiff was fairly obscure until after World War II when there was a revival of European interest. An imposing animal, it has been used by both the police and the army as a guard dog, though it is said to be fairly docile unless roused. The head appears even larger than it is because of the loose skin and massive wrinkle. The thick neck with heavy dewlaps is often emphasized by a traditional heavily studded collar. The ears are usually cropped to a small triangle. The height can be up to 75cm (29in) and the weight as much as 70kg (154lb). The short, glossy coat is usually blue-grey, black, brindle or mahogany.

## BULLDOG

The Bulldog, symbol of British tenacity, was developed for the sport of bull-baiting, which became popular in the Middle Ages. It required a strong, agile dog, tolerant of pain and careless of its own safety. Dogs with undershot jaws were preferred, as a grip where the lower teeth fitted tightly in front of the upper was very hard to break. In addition the lay back of the nostrils allowed the dog to breathe while still hanging on. Bulldogs nearly died out after the sport became illegal, but were saved by breeders who set about altering both the temperament and the shape. The coat can be any colour except black, black and white or black and tan. The weight is about 25kg (55lb).

## DOGUE DE BORDEAUX

The Dogue de Bordeaux is a giant, short-coated mastiff, with a history stretching back to the Romano-Gallic wars. Numbers fell severely during the food shortages in France in World War II. Modern breeders have concentrated on the breed's traits of affectionate loyalty rather than the ferocity required in the past. The dog now has a calm temperament and is very tolerant of children. The height can be an awe-inspiring 76cm (30in) and the weight can be 65.5kg (145lb). Colour can be golden, mahogany or any shade of fawn. White markings are permissible except on the head. Self-coloured dogs should have a black mask and ears.

## FRENCH BULLDOG

Great efforts were made in the 19th century to produce a toy Bulldog, and a number of these dogs were taken to France by emigrant workers. There they acquired some fame, particularly those with the big bat ears, which enhanced their clownish expression. Despite its fashionable appeal the large, erect ear carriage proved difficult to stabilize and the breed was really produced in a big way by US breeders at the start of this century. The Frenchie has an expression like a wistful comedian, with a good-humoured character to match. The colour can be brindle, pied or, in some countries, fawn. The height is 38cm (15in) and the ideal weight is about 12.5kg (28lb).

## BOSTON TERRIER

The Boston Terrier is one of the very few native North American breeds. It is a lively little dog, with a satin-smooth coat. Brindle or black is the main body colour and either must be highlighted by white markings, the position of which is very important in the show ring. The ears are naturally erect but are nevertheless cropped in the US. The weight can be up to 11.5kg (25lb), but dogs under 7kg (15lb) are most popular. The breed was reputedly developed by Boston coachmen who crossed the pedigree imported stock of their employers – including the Bulldog and some form of terrier – to create a new breed of their own.

# HOUNDS

The dog was first used by man as a hunting companion, for it was not only faster but possessed a much greater scenting ability than our own primitive ancestors. The hound group consists of hunting dogs and the history of some of these breeds can be traced back further than any others. Hounds themselves can be divided into sighthounds and those which hunt by scent. The sighthounds include the fastest of all dogs, for they are expected to overtake and pull down their quarry within a comparatively short distance. The instinct to chase a fast moving object is inborn in most dogs, but is particularly strong in the sighthounds. However, when they can no longer see the prey they quickly lose interest. Hounds which hunt by scent are much more persistent and do not need to be as fast, as their objective is to follow relentlessly and wear down their quarry. Stamina and a good nose are more important than speed.

**Whippet**

**Deerhound**

**Irish Wolfhound**

## WHIPPET
The Whippet is the fastest sprinter of all dogs, but it can be overtaken by the larger greyhound types after a short distance. Very small, toy greyhounds have a long history, but the medium-sized Whippet only emerged clearly in the 19th century, as a sporting dog favoured by the miners and mill workers of the north of England. It was used for rabbit coursing and racing before coming to the fore as a show dog and companion animal. The Whippet is an extremely elegant dog without being delicate in any way. The smooth coat of this breed can be almost any colour and the ideal height is 51cm (20in).

## DEERHOUND
The Deerhound is a Scottish breed, a dog of strength and speed which was expected to course and pull down the red deer of the Scottish highlands, a favourite sport of the clan chieftains and the lairds. In looks and character it remains an aristocrat as befits its history. The Deerhound has been known for 1,000 years, though nobody knows what the early dogs looked like. However, the breed has changed little over the past three centuries. Deerhounds make good companion animals, being gentle, good tempered and easy to train. The colour of the harsh, wiry coat is usually a dark, blue-grey. Wheaten and brindle Deerhounds are now seen only rarely. The minimum height is 76cm (30in) and the weight can be as much as 45.5kg (100lb).

## IRISH WOLFHOUND
The Irish Wolfhound is the tallest breed of dog in the world. The minimum height of this breed should be 79cm (31in) and dogs have been known to exceed this by as much as 20cm (8in). The ideal weight is 54.5kg (120lb). Despite its size and power, the Wolfhound should possess a graceful symmetry. The breed appears to be of Celtic origin and has been known since pre-Christian times. It was used in Ireland to hunt the Irish elk as well as the wolf and the boar. Legend has it that Wolfhounds accompanied Irish chieftains into battle and were capable of pulling an enemy from his horse. Colours include grey, brindle, black, pure white, fawn, and steel grey.

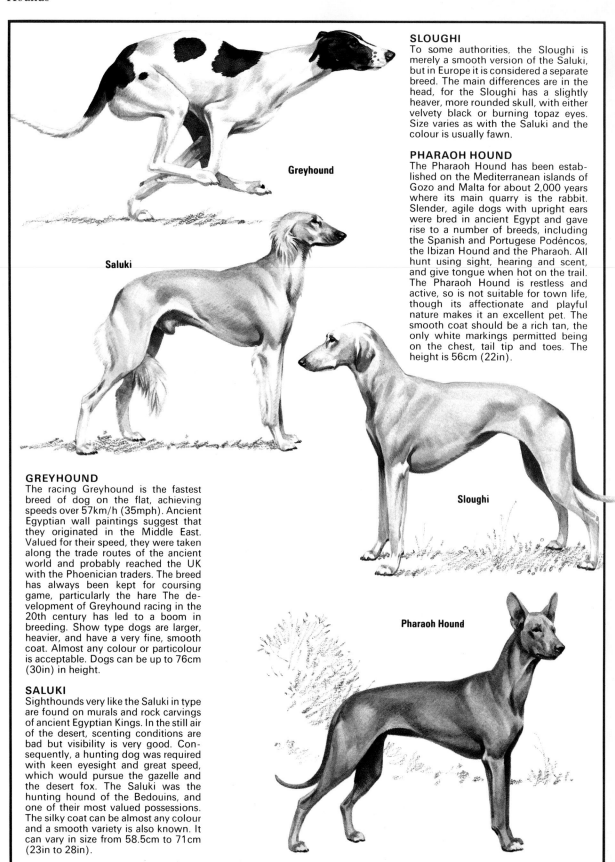

Greyhound

Saluki

## SLOUGHI

To some authorities, the Sloughi is merely a smooth version of the Saluki, but in Europe it is considered a separate breed. The main differences are in the head, for the Sloughi has a slightly heaver, more rounded skull, with either velvety black or burning topaz eyes. Size varies as with the Saluki and the colour is usually fawn.

## PHARAOH HOUND

The Pharaoh Hound has been established on the Mediterranean islands of Gozo and Malta for about 2,000 years where its main quarry is the rabbit. Slender, agile dogs with upright ears were bred in ancient Egypt and gave rise to a number of breeds, including the Spanish and Portugese Podéncos, the Ibizan Hound and the Pharaoh. All hunt using sight, hearing and scent, and give tongue when hot on the trail. The Pharaoh Hound is restless and active, so is not suitable for town life, though its affectionate and playful nature makes it an excellent pet. The smooth coat should be a rich tan, the only white markings permitted being on the chest, tail tip and toes. The height is 56cm (22in).

Sloughi

Pharaoh Hound

## GREYHOUND

The racing Greyhound is the fastest breed of dog on the flat, achieving speeds over 57km/h (35mph). Ancient Egyptian wall paintings suggest that they originated in the Middle East. Valued for their speed, they were taken along the trade routes of the ancient world and probably reached the UK with the Phoenician traders. The breed has always been kept for coursing game, particularly the hare The development of Greyhound racing in the 20th century has led to a boom in breeding. Show type dogs are larger, heavier, and have a very fine, smooth coat. Almost any colour or particolour is acceptable. Dogs can be up to 76cm (30in) in height.

## SALUKI

Sighthounds very like the Saluki in type are found on murals and rock carvings of ancient Egyptian Kings. In the still air of the desert, scenting conditions are bad but visibility is very good. Consequently, a hunting dog was required with keen eyesight and great speed, which would pursue the gazelle and the desert fox. The Saluki was the hunting hound of the Bedouins, and one of their most valued possessions. The silky coat can be almost any colour and a smooth variety is also known. It can vary in size from 58.5cm to 71cm (23in to 28in).

## IBIZAN HOUND

The Ibizan Hound takes its name from Ibiza, an island off the east coast of Spain. Isolation on a small island for centuries has ensured the purity of the breed. It is a large, very agile dog, able to jump great heights from a standing start. It hunts singly or in couples and will retrieve to hand, which is rare among hounds. The short coat, which can be smooth or rough, is white with either red or tawny markings. The height can be as much as 74cm (29in).

## AFGHAN HOUND

The Afghan, the coursing hound of the hill tribesmen, was used to hunt gazelle and small mountain deer. It first came to the notice of British army officers during border clashes between Afghanistan and India. However, stock from the dogs they brought back did not survive World War I and the breed was not established in the UK until the 1920s. The coat makes it a spectacular show dog for those willing to spend up to 15 hours preparing it for the show ring. It can be any colour. The height can be up to 74cm (29in), with weight about 29kg (64lb).

## BORZOI

The Borzoi is possibly the most aristocratic of the hounds, combining elegance with majesty. It was used in Russia for coursing wolves. The body is that of a galloping dog, but it should seem to have muscular strength as well as speed. The coat is long and silky and can be any colour. The Borzoi has an innate dignity and self-composure. Like many hounds, it has a mind of its own where obedience is concerned. The minimum height is 74cm (29in).

## BEAGLE

The Beagle is now one of the most popular pets on both sides of the Atlantic. As the height should not exceed 40.5cm (16in), it is a convenient size for modern living. The coat is short, smooth, and can be any mixture of colours except liver. The gaily carried tail is the hallmark of a breed that is always merry and bright. The Beagle originated in the UK where it is still used to hunt the hare. Both Queen Elizabeth I and Queen Victoria had packs of pocket Beagles, dogs about 25cm (10in) high which could still hunt well.

Ibizan Hound

Afghan Hound

Borzoi

Beagle

Basset Hound

## BASSET HOUND

The Basset Hound is a sociable animal and is widely kept as a pet. It is a large dog on short legs. Though the height is only 38cm (15in), the weight is 25kg (55lb). As its ancestors have been pack hounds for centuries, it does not adapt well to being alone and can voice its distress loudly. The doleful, serious look is misleading, for it is good natured and hearty, although, like most of the scent hounds, it can be obstinate. Bassett packs still hunt the hare in the traditional manner, being followed on foot. The working dogs have longer, straighter legs and fewer skin wrinkles.

**Foxhound**

## FOXHOUND

The Foxhound is bred solely to hunt the fox as speedily and efficiently as possible. It is never exhibited at shows held under Kennel Club regulations, and is totally unsuitable as a pet. Its life is that of a pack dog. It is kennelled, fed and worked in a pack, following the faintest of scents at the fastest of speeds. They are beautifully functional dogs, combining pace and power with well-balanced symmetry. The average height is about 61cm (24in).

## OTTERHOUND

The Otterhound is one of the rarest and most remarkable of British hounds. The dog has an exceptional nose and is expected to follow a waterborne scent, one of the most difficult tasks a hound can be asked to do. It is a very strong swimmer, totally indifferent to wet and cold. Otterhound packs in the UK were disbanded when the otter became a protected species and these hounds now appear in the show ring in the UK and the US. The coarse coat is usually grizzle or sandy. The height can be up to 68.5cm (27in) and the weight is about 40.5kg (90lb).

## BASSET ARTESIAN-NORMAND

Short-legged hunting dogs have a long history, for they were known in 2,000 BC. The name 'Basset' was first used in a 16th-century French book on hunting, and it is in France that several Basset breeds were developed. They have excellent noses and are tenacious. Their build enables them to force through thick cover and when on a line they are particularly melodious. The Basset Artesian-Normand is a powerful dog with a height of up to 35.5cm (14in). The smooth coat is either tan and white or tricolour.

**Otterhound**

**Petit Basset Griffon Vendeen**

**Basset Artesien-Normand**

**Miniature Wire-haired Dachshund**

**Standard Long-haired Dachshund**

**Standard Smooth-haired Dachshund**

## PETIT BASSET GRIFFON VENDEEN

The Petit Basset Griffon Vendeen is shown and kept as a pet both in its native France and elsewhere. A keen hunter, it is as happy on its own as it is in a pack. The shaggy coat is often grey and white or orange and white in colour. It is a particularly lively and friendly dog. The height is 38cm (15in).

## DACHSHUNDS

There are six breeds of Dachshund, distinguished by coat and size, for there are three different coat types and a standard and miniature breed in each. They are German in origin and were originally bred to hunt badgers and foxes underground. This required a long, sinewy body, a deep rib cage for heart and lung capactiy, broad paws for digging and a loud bark to let the huntsman know where the dog was underground. The **Standard Smooth-haired Dachshund** is probably the oldest of the breeds and one of the most popular. Given the chance, it is still an avid hunter, but is also a home- and comfort-loving creature. Dachshunds are greedy and need a strong-minded owner to prevent them becoming obese. The Standard Smooth-haired makes a good family dog and an effective watchdog. The three most popular colours are red, black and tan, and chocolate and tan. The ideal weight for Standard Dachshunds is 9–12kg (20–26lb). The **Standard Long-haired Dachshund** has the most glamorous coat, being soft, slightly wavy, and shiny. Long-haired Dachshunds are more reserved than the short-haired and also rather easier to train. The **Miniature Wire-haired Dachshund** is a bouncing extrovert of a dog. The coat, which may be brindle or dapple colouring, has to be stripped out two or three times a year. The ideal weight is 4.5kg (10lb).

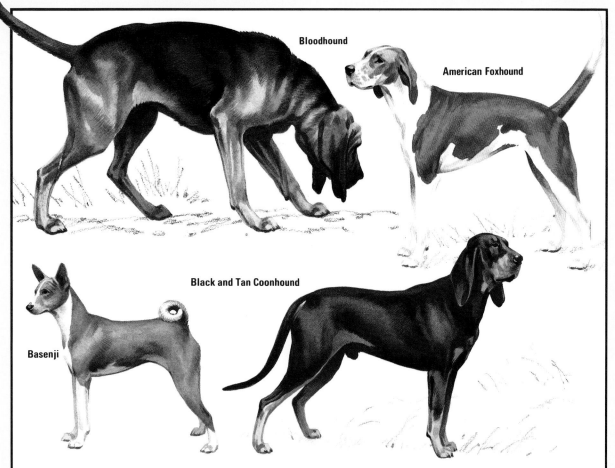

Bloodhound

American Foxhound

Black and Tan Coonhound

Basenji

## BLOODHOUND
The Bloodhound can follow older and fainter trails than any other breed. This ability has been used by police, though the dog is otherwise totally unsuited for police work, being sensitive and affectionate. The name refers to the breed's pure-blooded ancestry rather than its ferocity. The dog has loose, wrinkly skin on its face and neck. The colour is red or black and tan. It is 68.5cm (27in) high and weighs 50kg (110lb).

## AMERICAN FOXHOUND
Early American settlers who were men of substance took their hounds with them, and from these and later imports from France, Ireland and the UK evolved the American Foxhound. As well as hunting in a pack, this dog is used to hunt foxes singly with the gun. The height should be 63.5cm (25in) and the dog can be any colour.

## BLACK AND TAN COONHOUND
Racoon and opossum hunting is a popular sport in the southern states of the US. A number of breeds have been bred for this purpose, but the Black and Tan Coonhound is the only one recognised by the American Kennel Club. It is primarily a working dog, able to withstand extremes of climate and travel fast in rough terrain. The height is 68.5cm (27in).

## BASENJI
The Basenji, an African hunting dog, has the high head carriage of a dog that uses both sight and scent to hunt. The Basenji is unusual in that it cleans itself using paw and tongue like a cat, and does not bark. However, it is far from silent, making a sound between a chortle and a yodel. Red with white points is the most popular colour. The height should be 43cm (17in) and the weight 11kg (24lb).

## RHODESIAN RIDGEBACK
The Rhodesian Ridgeback is of South African origin. It was created by crossing the ridgebacked hunting dog of the Hottentot tribesman with European breeds to create a larger dog suitable for hunting big game. These dogs were nicknamed 'Lion Dogs', for they were expected to be courageous and agile enough to track and hold at bay animals up to and including the size of lions. The distinctive ridge of hair grows in the reverse direction to the rest of the coat. The coat colour is red wheaten. Dogs should weigh about 36kg (80lb) with a height of 68.5cm (27in).

Rhodesian Ridgeback

# SPITZ GROUP

The spitz breeds tend to be stockily built and rather square in outline. The head is usually wedge-shaped and the ears are pointed and erect. The coat is dense and often stands off from the body and the bushy tail is carried over the back. Spitz breeds are distributed worldwide from the Far East to the Arctic Circle and this suggests that they are one of the basic types of dog. This view is supported by archeological evidence from Europe showing that the dogs accompanying Neolithic Man were of a spitz type, and also by the general appearance of the modern dog which suggests less divergence from a wolf-like ancestor than many other groups of breeds. The spitz breeds are often strong-willed and independent, but their adaptability makes them versatile working dogs.

### ALASKAN MALAMUTE
The Alaskan Malamute is descended from the sledge dogs used by the Mahlemut Eskimos both to haul loads over the frozen tundra and carry packs over mountainous terrain. The breed has adapted well to more temperate climates but as a pet it needs a lot of exercise and firm training. As with all the Arctic sledge dogs, it has a double coat. The well-furred tail covers the feet and nose when the dog is curled up in the snow to keep it warm and dry. The height and weight can be up to 71cm (28in) and 56kg (125lb). The coat is usually grey with white on the underparts. Head markings give either a cap- or mask-like effect.

### JAPANESE AKITA
The Akita is the best known of Japan's five spitz breeds and also the country's national dog. It dates back more than 300 years and was formerly used for hunting large game such as wild boar. It was later used in Japan for police and army work. The dog was brought to the West by US servicemen who had occupied Japan after World War II. The Akita is said to be affectionate and easily trained. All colours are acceptable, but they should be brilliant and clear. The height can be as much as 71cm (28in).

### GREENLAND HUSKY
While the Arctic belonged only to the Eskimo and Indian, each isolated nomadic tribe had its own type of husky. When the Arctic became of interest to the white man, particularly during the Yukon gold rush, any animal that was large enough to haul a sledge suddenly became valuable. This led to so much cross-breeding to meet the demand for huskies that very few of the pure types have survived. One that remains relatively untouched is the Greenland Husky, owing to a ban on the import of dogs into Greenland. There is no restriction on colour, but black and white is the most usual. The height is about 61cm (24in).

Alaskan Malamute

Japanese Akita

Greenland Husky

## SIBERIAN HUSKY

The most popular and widely known of the huskies is the Siberian Husky. Its comparatively moderate build provides more speed without any loss of stamina. The breed comes from the north-eastern region of Siberia where it was bred by the Chukchi tribe who used the dogs both for pulling sledges and for hunting and herding. This background is reflected in the dog's character today, for it is friendly and tractable, although it needs a lot of exercise. The Siberian Husky made its first impact in the US in the sport of sledge-dog racing. It has won the All-Alaska Sweepstakes repeatedly since its inception in 1908. The Siberian Husky Club of America has always encouraged owners to race their dogs in an effort to ensure that the working capabilities of the breed are not lost in the show ring stock. One remarkable feature of the breed is that the eyes can be any shade of blue or brown. The coat colour is usually grey with white under-parts and cap- or mask-like markings on the head are common. The height is 60cm (23in).

## SAMOYED

Despite the fluffy appearance the outer coat of the Samoyed should be harsh in texture. The thick, soft undercoat helps the coarser top coat to stand off from the body. Though the dog is usually silvery white (cream and biscuit shades are also allowed), the animal is not too difficult to keep clean since dirt when dry should brush off easily from a correctly textured coat. A certain in-dependence of outlook is common to most spitz breeds, but the Samoyed standard also requires that the dog should display affection. Perhaps to emphasize this, the Samoyed has an engaging and characteristic grin caused by a slight upward turn of the black lips when the mouth is open. The breed originally came from northern Russia where the Samoyed people used it for herding reindeer as well as for haulage. The height should be about 56cm (22in) and the weight about 25kg (55lb).

## KARELIAN BEAR DOG

The Karelian Bear Dog is now more used for hunting elk and deer than bear, since the latter have become rare in Finland. It is a medium-sized, sturdy dog with an excellent nose and was considered to have a special aptitude for finding the bear's winter lair. The colour is black with white markings and the dog has the usual double coat of all the northern spitz breeds. Combings of the soft woolly undercoat are spun and made into mittens and hats. The dog has to be exceptionally courageous but it is also aggressive with other dogs, and distrustful of strangers. The fierce-ness and stubborness of character which make it a good hunting dog are also an effective bar to its greater popularity. The height can be up to 61cm (24in).

Siberian Husky

Samoyed

Karelian Bear Dog

Finnish Spitz

## FINNISH SPITZ

The Finnish Spitz looks one of the most fox-like of dogs mainly because of its colouring, which should be a clear and brilliant red. The shade of red may vary from dog to dog, but a dirty or muddy colour is considered most objection-able. The outer coat should be short and close on the face and legs, longer on the body and longer still on the neck, shoulders and tail. The colour lightens on the underparts of the dog. This is a hunting dog and is still widely used as such in Finland mainly to find game birds such as capercaillie and grouse. The dog is expected to flush the bird into a tree and indicate its position by continous barking. It is an alert, lively, active dog with a strong homing in-stinct. Suspicious of strangers, the Fin-nish Spitz can be a noisy and effective watchdog. The height is 50cm (20in) and the weight 16kg (36lb).

## CHOW CHOW

The Chow Chow has a number of unique features: the bluish-black tongue and mouth cavity, the stilted hind movement produced by a hindleg that is almost straight, and the characteristic scowling expression. The Chow Chow is aloof, silent and responds only to those it trusts. The dog must be whole-coloured and is usually red, though black and blue are also quite common. There is a smooth variety. The height is 56cm (22in). The Chow Chow originated in China where it was used for a range of purposes, including hunting and guarding, and as a sledge dog. At one time it was bred for its fur and fattened for the table. It reached the West in the 18th century.

## KEESHOND

The Keeshond, from the Netherlands, has also been known as the Dutch Barge Dog, for spitz of this type travelled with the cargo boats of the waterways. They were also kept by small farmers as general working dogs. The name is thought to have come from that of Kees de Gyzelaar, the leader of the Dutch Patriots party at the end of the 18th century. He owned a spitz of this type which became the people's symbol. The colour is wolf or silver grey with shading, and a cream undercoat. The lighter face markings give the appearance of spectacles around the eyes. The height is 46cm (18in).

## SCHIPPERKE

The Schipperke comes from the Flemish areas of Belgium. The name means 'Little Skipper' for the dog was often carried on canal boats to act as a watchdog and keep down the rats and mice. It is said that a tailless dog was preferred as wagging tails were liable to knock things overboard. Like many spitz, this breed has dignity and independence, combined with an intense loyalty to those they know and a distrust of strangers. The European Schipperke must be black, but other whole colours are accepted elsewhere. The dense, harsh coat forms a mane on the neck. The weight is about 7kg (15lb).

## ELKHOUND

The Elkhound is the national breed of Norway where a similar dog has been known since Viking times. It is independent in outlook but will respect and obey understanding authority and should be friendly and sensible. The coat is grey, with black tips on the outer coat giving an attractive shaded effect. The ideal height is 52cm (20in) and the weight 22.5kg (50lb).

## NORWEGIAN BUHUND

This is one of the smaller spitz breeds as the height should not exceed 45cm (17¾in). It is a lightly built, well-balanced dog. The outer coat is harsh and the colour can be biscuit, black, red or wolf sable. The Buhund should be a courageous and alert dog with a natural herding instinct.

Chow Chow

Keeshond

Schipperke

Elkhound

Norwegian Buhund

# TERRIERS

Many of the breeds in the terrier group were developed to 'go to earth' and follow their quarry underground. The name 'terrier' comes from the Latin word 'terra' meaning earth. The majority of terrier breeds originated in the UK though little is known of their early history as they were very localized in type. This is shown in many of the breed names which are those of places. A dog admired for its working ability might sire many puppies in its own neighbourhood, in this way building up a local strain of dogs all similar in appearance. It was little more than a century ago that some of these strains were recognised and established as purebred. Though there is a great variety of size and colour among the terrier breeds, they are all distinguished by their energy, hardy constitutions and courage, often in the face of great odds.

**Airedale Terrier**

## AIREDALE TERRIER
The Airedale, often called the 'King of the Terriers', is the largest breed of this group and can stand 61cm (24in). It was originally bred in the valley of the River Aire, Yorkshire, probably to hunt otters. Obviously it was not expected to go underground. The dog should have a keen and alert expression. As with a number of terrier breeds, the head resembles an oblong shoe box. The coat should be straight, hard and wiry, and much skill is needed to trim a show dog. The colour is black or dark grizzle, with tan head and legs.

## BEDLINGTON TERRIER
The mild, lamb-like appearance of the Bedlington is deceptive. When the dog is roused, the small, bright eyes flash full of fire. The breed is built to move speedily to the elusive rabbit rather than push it out from an underground lair. The name comes from a Northumbrian village where the breed was first established about 1820. The thick coat is either pale blue or pale liver. The height is about 41cm (16in) and the weight 10.5kg (23lb).

## LAKELAND TERRIER
Fox hounds in the fell country of the north of England are accompanied on foot as the terrain is unsuitable for horses. With the hounds go terriers, fast enough to keep up, but agile and wiry enough to creep into rocky crevices or crawl underground after their quarry they have either to dislodge or to kill. This is the background of the Lakeland Terrier. The most popular colour is red grizzle. The weight should be about 7.5kg (17lb) and the height about 35.5cm (14in).

## BULL TERRIER
The Bull Terrier is an agile and muscular heavyweight. The standard sets no height and weight limits, merely calling for a dog with the maximum of substance for its size. The distinctive head has tremendous jaw power. The dog was bred from bulldog and terrier crosses in the early 19th century. The aim was to produce dogs that had the courage and disregard of pain of the bull-baiting breeds and the speed and agility of terriers, which could be matched in dog fighting contests. Bull Terriers can be white or coloured.

**Lakeland Terrier**

**Bedlington Terrier**

**Bull Terrier**

**Border Terrier**

**Smooth Fox Terrier**

**Wire Fox Terrier**

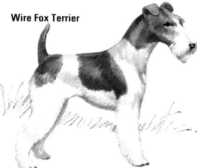

**Manchester Terrier**

**Staffordshire Bull Terrier**

## BORDER TERRIER

The Border Terrier originally came from the Northumberland/Scottish border, where it was bred as a working hunt terrier used to bolt foxes from their earths for waiting hounds. As it is required to work in unison with other terriers as well as foxhounds, the breed tends to be less aggressive with other dogs and less excitable than other terriers. It is, however, courageous and tough with a natural instinct to chase and kill, so it must be taught what is legitimate quarry and what is forbidden. The weight is about 7kg (15lb) giving a terrier that is active enough to follow a horse yet small enough to go to ground. The standard calls for the head to resemble that of an otter and there are certainly similarities in the depth and breadth of skull and muzzle. The short, wiry coat, needs only a little tidying for the dog to be in show condition. Colour can be wheaten or grizzle and may have tan markings.

## SMOOTH FOX TERRIER

The Smooth Fox Terrier was bred to hunt the fox but, like the Wire Fox Terrier, it has left its working background far in the past. It has been suggested that huntsmen in some districts preferred a predominantly white terrier as it was easier to distinguish from its natural quarry the fox, and so both Smooth and Wire Fox Terriers are mainly white with tan or black patches. As soon as the first dog shows took place in England, in the 1860s, Smooth Fox Terriers were used as show dogs. The breed type was refined and stabilized to produce a smart and stylish terrier. It became one of the most popular of all dogs at the beginning of this century, but has since attracted little attention. The coat is flat and hard in texture, and is easy to keep clean and care for. The Smooth Fox Terrier weighs about 8kg (18lb).

## WIRE FOX TERRIER

Both the Wire and the Smooth Fox Terrier developed from the same basic stock, but little is known about either before they reached the show ring and became exhibition animals. The Wire Fox Terrier achieved its greatest popularity in the 1920s and 1930s when it became the top ranking terrier and one of the most widely kept of pedigree breeds. At its best it epitomzed the terrier virtues of alertness, energy and enthusiasm. At its worst, it was noisy, over excitable and aggressive towards other dogs, faults which are typical of the terrier group. Both Wire and Smooth Fox Terriers should be about the same size, 39.5cm (15in). The coat of the Wire is its distinguishing feature. It should be double with the dense, wiry outer hair being cushioned by a finer undercoat. Professional trimming gives the dog its immaculate, square-cut outline.

## MANCHESTER TERRIER

A black and tan terrier has existed in the UK for more than 200 years. The wirehaired version became extinct more than a century ago. The smooth version was kept for fighting and for vermin killing. In particular it was matched in the rat pits where wagers were laid on how many rats a dog could kill in a specified time. This gambling sport was popular in the Manchester area and gradually the name Manchester Terrier became the official one. The Manchester has a racy outline, which suggests that the dog was used for rabbiting as well as ratting. Like other smooth-coated terriers it needs a warm, dry bed and is fond of its own comfort. The glossy black coat and the striking tan markings should have made the breed popular, but this has never happened. Possibly it is because the dark eyes set in the required wedge-shaped black head give the dog a somewhat hard expression. The height should be about 40.5cm (16in).

## STAFFORDSHIRE BULL TERRIER

The so-called sport of dog fighting has been carried out in many parts of the world. Though now generally illegal, clandestine meetings were held in many places long after governments had outlawed the activity. The Staffordshire Bull Terrier is a survival from the past, the nearest breed to those who were matched in the dog pits to see which one would have the courage to last out or kill its opponent. The breed was not recognized in the show ring until 1935. Its stronghold has always been in the Staffordshire area of England where the miners and steel workers wanted the toughest of dogs. Like a number of other breeds not trustworthy with other members of the same breed, the Staffordshire has a friendly temperament towards humans and is very tolerant of children. The short coat can be almost any colour. The height and weight can be up to 40.5cm (16in) and 17¼kg (38lb).

Welsh Terrier

Scottish Terrier

Dandie Dinmont Terrier

Norfolk Terrier

Norwich Terrier

## WELSH TERRIER

A rough-coated, black and tan terrier is known to have existed from the 17th century onwards. The English version of this terrier became extinct within a couple of centuries and it seems likely that the Welsh Terrier is the nearest surviving relative of a type that disappeared completely elsewhere. There are obvious similarities between the Welsh and Lakeland Terrier, but the Welsh is rather stockier in build and the black and tan colouring is much deeper and brighter in shade. The Welsh Terrier should be an affectionate extrovert. It is not as noisy or pugnacious as some breeds and is a convenient size for town or country life. The coarse, wiry coat needs trimming periodically. The height should be about 39.5cm (15in) and the weight about 9.5kg (21lb).

## SCOTTISH TERRIER

Owing to the isolation of the Highlands of Scotland, many local types of terrier have been developed. Since they have all come from Scotland, they are all called Scotch Terriers, and all once competed against each other at dog shows. In 1882 a standard was drawn up for the Scottish Terrier that sharply differentiated it from the Dandies, the Skyes and the Cairns which were also shown in the Scotch Terrier classes. The standard calls for a thickset dog with a head long for its size. The dog is now too thickset for its original job of going to ground and it is also heavily barbered to get the correct show outline. In temperament the Scottie tends to be a self-contained dog, a little dour with strangers and distinctly peppery towards other dogs. Wheaten and brindle, as well as black, are acceptable colours. The height should be about 28cm (11in) and the weight about 10.5kg (23lb).

## DANDIE DINMONT TERRIER

The Dandie Dinmont is one of the most distinctive of the terriers, a low-set dog of graceful curves and sinewy strength, and a head that is proportionately large. The dog has a look of dignity and determination. The domed forehead is covered with soft, silky hair. The tail,

carried like a scimitar, complements the undulating backline. The coat is about 5cm (2in) long and feels crisp to the touch. The colour phases of the Dandie are called pepper and mustard. Pepper Dandies are shades of grey while the mustards vary from reddish brown to pale fawn. The height should be about 28cm (11in) and the weight is about 11kg (24lb). The Dandie is still occasionally used for the job it was bred for, that of bolting the fox.

## NORFOLK TERRIER

The only difference between the Norfolk and the Norwich is that the former has drop ears and the latter carries its ears erect. The dogs share the same background and history. They were bred together in the show ring under the title Norwich until 1964. In that year, the English Kennel Club acted on the advice of Norwich breeders and

allowed the two types to separate, the drop-eared variety becoming known as the Norfolk Terrier.

## NORWICH TERRIER

The Norwich is one of the smallest of the terriers, a compact bundle of energy with a rough-textured jacket which is usually red; other colours include black and tan and grizzle. The height should not be more than 25.5cm (10in). The short legs and powerful hindquarters are aids to both digging and forcing its way into narrow undergound passages. The breed comes from East Anglia and, though it was not recognized until 1923, there are plenty of 19th-century oil paintings showing that a similar type of dog existed for at least a century before that. It is a hardy, adaptable and easy-going little dog. Its coat is quite heavy for its size and almost forms a mane round its neck.

### IRISH TERRIER

The jaunty, self-assured Irish Terrier has the nickname of 'Dare Devil'. It is a keen, alert dog, inquisitive, and ever ready to avenge an insult from any other dog. Small, dark eyes with a wicked glint give the desired varminty expression The dog is self-coloured, and bright red, red-wheaten, or yellow-red are the most desirable shades. The hard, wiry and straight coat needs stripping out several times a year if the dog is to remain smart. The ideal height is 48cm (18in).

### WEST HIGHLAND WHITE TERRIER

The West Highland White is now one of the best known of the terriers. However, 100 years ago, when they appeared in Cairn litters they were often drowned at birth as undesirable. Their future was secured by a Scottish family who felt that white dogs were more easily seen when were working among the rocks and heather. Ironically, Westies became a breed in their own right before the Cairn itself was recognised. The harsh, white coat requires some trimming. The height should be 28cm (11in).

### CAIRN TERRIER

The Cairn Terrier was given its present name in 1910, although the same dog existed for a century before this. It was widely used in western Scotland to bolt quarry such as otters and polecats from the tumbled heaps of stone called cairns. A sturdy, rugged dog, it is perfectly adapted to search among rocks, wriggle into crevices and burrow under obstructions. The colour includes all shades of red and grey. The height is about 31cm (12in) and the weight about 7.5kg (16lb).

### SEALYHAM TERRIER

The Sealyham Terrier, from Wales, is named after the estate owned by a Captain Edwardes, who first bred them. He wanted a courageous dog that was also the right shape for tackling foxes and badgers underground. The Sealyham is a dog of character that will repay a firm owner with affection. The hard, wiry coat, which needs much trimming, should be white; the head and ears may have coloured markings. The maximum height is 30.5cm (12in) and the weight should be about 9kg (20lb).

### SKYE TERRIER

The Skye Terrier is the most glamorous dog in the terrier group. The hair reaches the ground, making a sweeping coat round the dog. It is a very long and low-to-ground dog. A great hunter, it has been known as a vermin killer on the island of Skye for about 400 years. The Skye is a one-man dog, distrustful of strangers. Colours include dark or light grey, fawn or cream with black points. Though the height should be 25.5cm (10in), the dog can be as much as 103cm (41in) long. It should weigh 11.5kg (25lb).

Irish Terrier

Cairn Terrier

West Highland White Terrier

Sealyham Terrier

Skye Terrier

## KERRY BLUE TERRIER

The Kerry Blue Terrier is indigenous to the south-west of Ireland. It was kept as a general working dog. Among other things, it was expected to dig out foxes, catch rats, and round up cattle. The modern dog should show alert determination and disciplined gameness. Dogs are born black and the desired shade of blue does not come until maturity. The well-groomed look of the show Kerry is produced by sculpting the coat with scissors. The most desirable weight is 16.5kg (37lb) and the height is about 49.5cm (19.5cm).

## CESKY TERRIER

The Cesky Terrier is a recent sporting breed developed in Czechoslovakia. The colour phases of the coat suggest that it was created by crossing the Dandie Dinmont with other short-legged terriers such as the Sealyham. The coat is silky and wavy, and usually either grey-blue or light coffee-brown in colour. The Cesky is a keen hunter, but is also said to be good-natured and affectionate. Show dogs are trimmed to have a forelock and whiskers. The height is 34kg (13in) and the weight 9kg (20lb).

## AMERICAN PIT BULL TERRIER

The name American Pit Bull Terrier gives the clue to this dog's origins, for it was bred for fighting and stems from the same Bull and Terrier crosses that produced the English Bull Terrier and the Staffordshire Bull Terrier. The American dog is bigger than either of these, standing 48.5cm (19in) high and weighing 27kg (60lb). The well-developed cheek muscles indicate a powerful bite. The ears are cropped and the coat is usually red or brindle.

## SOFT-COATED WHEATEN TERRIER

The Soft-coated Wheaten Terrier is also a native of southern Ireland. Like the Kerry blue, to which it was related, it was used as a cattle dog and vermin killer. The Wheaten should be a good-tempered dog, full of confidence and humour. It is about the same size as the Kerry Blue. The abundant coat should flow or fall naturally. Puppies are born dark and the coat lightens to the shade of ripening wheat as they mature. It should be a natural terrier, whose coat should not be over-trimmed or too stylized.

## AUSTRALIAN TERRIER

The Australian Terrier emerged as a breed in its own right about a century ago. Its origins are unclear, although it obviously owes something to the Yorkshire Terrier. The breed is fairly quiet with an affectionate nature. Active and agile, it is adept at killing vermin and has a reputation for snake killing. The harsh, straight coat is either blue and tan or sandy. There is a silky topknot on the head, which is a lighter shade. The height is about 25.5cm (10in) and the weight about 6.5kg (14lb).

Kerry Blue Terrier

Cesky Terrier

American Pit Bull Terrier

Australian Terrier

Soft-coated Wheaten Terrier

# INDEX